Penny Scryer

**Penny Stocks
Beginners Trading Bible**

Copyright ©2013
Lance K. Cruz Phromnopavong

All rights reserved, including the
rights to reproduce this work in any
form whatsoever,
Without any written
Permission from the publisher.
Self-Published:
Amazon.com/Create Space
By: L.K. Cruz P
Also
Author
of
Alchemical Whispers

Intro:

My name is lance I am a fashion designer by trade and penny stock as a business to fuel my fashion line but also a chance to have retirement security if I am lucky on picks.

I started paper trading (virtual money account) in 2008 and opened a real money account in 2009. I got a couple trades and had no idea what I was doing. That is the purpose of this book so you can avoid the head aches as well.

Once upon a trade…

I got a few thousand shares in **LVLT** *Level 3 Communications* I got in under a penny per share. Now not knowing what I was doing I sold on Emotion. That was my **big mistake**!

You see when it hit $1.90 per share I closed out all my holdings. Two weeks later the price per share soared to $23.00 per share. If I would have waited or better knew what I was doing I would have made $11,000.00 return on a $200 investment. Yes, I regret it but I learned a lot from that experience. I realized One important thing!

Mind Set:

I know this may sound weird. But to be successful at trading full time is treat it like a business. My Friend Emerald Waters; says to keep a **ZEN** mind set.

What I mean by this is you need to be stable to make smart effective trades, if you use irrational techniques and think stocks are a gamble then chances are you will lose your money.

I think with Zen trading in mind and treating trading itself as an art form or meditation, you will gain more pleasure and financial gains.

Now I am not saying take all your credit cards max them out and buy stocks, you have to be realistic, that is my point. =) . Only under no circumstances **ONLY invest money** that you are **willing to lose**.

When surfing the web for Penny Stock picks you might come across forums. While a lot of the forums are informative there is also lot of politics in the Penny Stock game.

I am not trying to sound crazy but you will find especially in penny stocks land there is lots of bashing going on, and lots of Pumping.

The key is doing your own research. No one on the Web is trying to save you from losing money. Legend has it that these Bashers are just pissed because they either get paid by post, or are just trying to push prices down for a good entry point.

Whatever the case may be haven't met an honest basher yet. And I have personally lost more money listening to them; rather than listening to my own "DD" (due diligence- researching the company and assets before investing).

Anyways, these forums are a great place to get ideas of which symbols to research. That's why mind set is important. Do not let anyone break your focus, or put you down for wanting to trade Penny Stocks.

The thing with Penny stocks is it is a Huge Risk, but Big Rewards for the right plays. Of course you have to make sure you're not getting sucked into a pump and dump Scheme.

Don't Fall In Love:

I hear this sometimes and I; disagree. **"Don't fall in love with a penny stock"** never hold long. I call BULLshit. I am Long on a few plays and if I was in Google when it was 60cent per share, I would still be holding long even though bashers were saying it would never fly.

If you like the shares then you must keep in mind that they will raise, I would hold long. If you think it's just a quick flip, then at 20% flip half of it and move on. The truth is there is now right way to trade stocks.

Important Skills:

Understanding fundamentals and having a basic understanding of contracts, share structure and financials I don't really care for since I am a chart type.

Learning Basic charting skills will dramatically help the way you trade. But some people prefer to trade off fundamentals rather than charts.

Whatever option is better for you over time and with experience a natural flow will start to dawn on you. You will then realize your trading style. Meditate and Research, develop an exit strategy or set a goal and stop loss.

There are lots of ways to balance out your portfolio; I

won't get into that because I am not a licensed financial advisor.
But I do well trading stocks.

Starting with penny stocks then moving into dividends I want to explore the world of Options but not until I have a secured sizable amount of dry powder ready.

Brokerage Account:

I myself prefer a cash account. Some people like margin account but that can cost you in the long run, since you are being matched by house money on some trades. Which you might later get billed for or pay higher taxes on.

There are a lot of brokerage firms to choose from but look for ones that do OTC and regular stocks, since you might want to trade penny stocks and regular ones.

Do your research each one has different pricing for all your trading needs. All the information is easily obtained on the web for free.

Be Patient:

Companies take time to build momentum does not freak out and panic sell, you may miss out on good trades.

Some traders are one tick flippers and 20%ers every 20% they cash out. But I am a Long I like to get the most out of my return.

In fact how I am funding my trade account is by having an online job writing articles. I get paid for every article I

write weekly and it goes into my brokerage account.
I think it's pretty brilliant. There are tons of writing jobs online and they are great because you can write them at your own pace.

Especially if you are trading penny stocks, at triple zero range, you are basically making 300,000 shares every 3 articles you write.

Because you can set up an ach from PayPal to your account some brokerage firms also offer in house bank accounts. Like *Scottrade,* for example.

The Big Question:

How do I make money on penny stocks? A lot of you may be asking this question, but so have I. it took me a long while to figure out a system good for me and develop my sense of trade style Kung Fu.

I started with 250$ and got some share for 0.0002 per

share. That came to be about 750,000shares total.

When the stock went up months later I sold half of my holdings and found 2 other plays and bought equal amount of shares in the two new plays. When those play raises above 75% I cashed out half and continued the cycle. Until I am holding, 10 plays.

I will leave the rest to your imagination since that's once you get these basic principles down you should by then find your trading style Kung Fu.

You can you chars to see trends and stuff, on your trading platform. Use your time wisely to find great entry points. Also when you get capitol up it might be a good idea to diversify your portfolio by adding some high dividend paying plays. Having multiple dividend paying plays is kind of like having insurance, you are rest assured you are getting a good ROI (return on investment).

Depending on how many shares you're holding, the dividend checks could be pretty large at times paid quarterly with a raise.

Charts can give you a forecast while you are scrying the world of pennies. Though there are many ways to read them a good thing to learn is support and resistance lines, so you can see the trends. There are plenty of free charting sources online for you to learn. There is also software but the tech is not always savvy.

Balls deep.

Take a chance. Why not? 100$ could make you 1,000 or more return. That's how some stocks roll if you get lucky. 4300% gains are not uncommon in penny land, but neither are scams.

Thankfully the SEC protects us as much as they can, by cracking down on these fake plays. In any rate if you timing is on point you will be guaranteed to make bank!

Hold for at least 3 days!

Nobody wants an account restriction, so always wait until your shares or funds clear before you sell off any recent buys. My favorite trading days are Tuesday and Fridays, I don't know why but it is.

The point is that at any point of sale, make sure you are making at least 20% back of your invested cashed into profits in cash or shares. Because if you sell 300,000 shares and gain 600,000 shares in return I see that as being profits as well. Because in one tick you just made back 40%

There is a Method though, here Quoted from famous V/r Sterling's 200-200,000 $ Process. It's great if you put it into practice and the formula works if one remains disciplined in the art of Zen Trading.

It doesn't matter what strategy you are using because you can implement this formula and adapt it to your Kung Fu Trades.

The "$200 to $200,000 Transformation Process"

Stock 1 = $200 to $400
Stock 2 = $400 to $800
Stock 3 = $800 to $1,600
Stock 4 = $1,600 to $3,200
Stock 5 = $3,200 to $6,400
Stock 6 = $6,400 to $12,800
Stock 7 = $12,800 to 25,600
Stock 8 = $25,600 to $51,200
Stock 9 = $51,200 to $102,400
Stock 10 = $102,400 to $204,800

V.R.Sterling

It will be important for you to remain disciplined and flexible to know when to move on. You might have to make the call to risk selling above 100% gains or selling at the 50% level for gains, or lower. You might even have to make the decision to pick a percentage drop to cut your losses to move on to a better opportunity. I will not make any decisions for anyone as everyone must be responsible for their own decisions for buying and selling. All I can do is share my thoughts that should be considered speculative in nature.

Something else to note, the higher you go up in money, the better the fundamentals you should be considering to minimize your risk; the choice is yours. Still, other variables will definitely have to be weighed whether to cut your losses and move on or to remain past your 100% gain as risk will always be a very important variable up for consideration. The key thing to consider here is the concept of remaining discipline as profits are achieved.

It doesn't really matter what process you use; either the $200 to $200,000 process or whatever to your desire. Let's use as another yet more conservative example where you take $10,000 and set your goals to make 20% return on 2 stocks per month for a total of 20% made on 24 stocks for the year. Let's go one step further and figure you would use only major market stocks although using penny stocks still could be used under your discretion. Some would consider this to be less risky. Your 20% gains from a minimum of 24 stocks would look like the table:

The "$10,000 from 20% from 24 Stocks Transformation Process"

Stock 1 = $10,000 to $12,000
Stock 2 = $12,000 to $14,400
Stock 3 = $14,400 to $17,280
Stock 4 = $17,280 to $20,736
Stock 5 = $20,736 to $24,883
Stock 6 = $24,883 to $29,860
Stock 7 = $29,860 to 25,600
Stock 8 = $25,600 to $38,832
Stock 9 = $35,832 to $42,998

Stock 10 = $42,998 to $51,598
Stock 11 = $51,598 to $61,918
Stock 12 = $61,918 to $74,302
Stock 13 = $74,302 to $89,162
Stock 14 = $89,162 to $106,994
Stock 15 = $106,994 to $128,393
Stock 16 = $128,393 to $150,472
Stock 17 = $150,472 to $180,566
Stock 18 = $180,566 to 216,679
Stock 19 = $216,679 to $260,015
Stock 20 = $260,015 to $312,018
Stock 21 = $312,018 to $374,422
Stock 22 = $374,422 to $449,306
Stock 23 = $449,306 to $539,167
Stock 24 = $539,167 to $647,000

V. R. Sterling

Imagine the possibilities this isn't easy. It takes patience and discipline. The moment you start to feel angry get up and walk away from the screen.

You have no control over the market and market makers…lol. But you do have your own mind and knowledge of charts.

Now you have an idea of what needs to be done to make this work as a business, not a gamble!

Stock Options:

For most of us the word "Options" is a scary adventure, but I recently started trading options. I for my strategy and budget prefer 22-50 day call option OTM or ITM strikes depending on the chart and try to keep in plays that have a delta of .40 or higher.

Call Options are nice because if the price of the stock goes higher than the price of the strike then your gains have unlimited potential.

Stock options give you the right to buy but not obligation.

This is what options are about you are buying a contract that gives you the right to lock in 100 shares at a certain price, so if you buy a 2.50 strike and the PPS goes up to 15$.

You as a trader may choose to exercise your option and pay 250$ for 100 shares instead of 1500$ or you can sell your contract for a premium 15$x100shares (1) contract =1500$ - commission and price of contract.

Let's just say you paid 10$ for your 2.50 strike your profit would average out to be in the $1400 profit off the premium range depending on your broker.
Options are a higher risk but better rewards if you are on point with your picks.

Options are a great way to leverage your portfolio as there are many strategies involved. With unlimited gains potential on the buying call side and unlimited loss on the puts.

It's important to do your research if you want to make money.

It is like a full time job not just easy cash if you want to be a successful trader. There are plenty of references online to help you learn strategies on different option trading styles.

Keep in mind Options do expire as to why I play Call options because if I buy a put its like shorting stocks if the strike price does not hit then you might end up paying margin fees. I made that mistake but lucked out at only having to pay 65$.

OTC markets do not offer options trading that I am aware of. So you will have to scan stocks like "S" Sprint.

Travel Safe Cashopper:

Some good smart phone apps you can get are stock spy for news and PR on time every time. Also if you type "stock" in the search of the app bar then it's easy to see what's available and you can see what fits your investing needs.

 Like I said before, a lot of great information is on the web free and trading software on the market is good but nothing works better than your brain.

 What's the fun if your computer does all of your work for you…trading is more than just a skill apparently it is a life style. A couple thousand dollars invested could make you six figures but you could also lose that couple thousand if you are not careful.

I suggest studying websites like investopiedia, barchart.com, and others along those lines. Tons of great content of stock, investing, etc. tutorials to help guide you understand the core of trading basics.

The main thing is take your time and maintain the K.I.S.S. principle. Kiss as in "keep it simple stupid" you won't go wrong, if you don't rush and take time to see the full picture of what options you have and actions you can take right in front of you.

Are you willing to sacrifice 25- 50% of your hottest stocks, to get triple the amount of shares you sell. Keep a watchful eye for plays that will correlate with each other so you are able to shift your portfolio if needed.

The main thing is don't get scared and if you are a scared person do not trade stocks. Especially penny stocks…they are not for the weak hearted.

I say this because though there is a lot of money in the penny underground, you have to know you're not in a pump and dump, and if you are… You have to be fearless.

But once you master the art of Penny Kung Fu, and can withstand blows of any fluctuation because you have a few hundred or thousand on the line, then you may be worthy of joining this magical world of stocks.

Unlike Wall Street the OTC market is a tight network of traders; we work together and defend our mindfully placed investments from bashers. Seriously do these guys get paid to talk shit I don't know?

But no matter what kind of bullshit they throw it doesn't seem to shake the most savvy of penny stock celebrities. So keep that in mind if you enter penny stock forums.

If someone hypes a stock research it before u jump all in. as some pumpers are just trying to rid of their last shares. But, sometimes you get lucky and swoop into a future hot play months in advanced, thinking you're stuck in a shitty play but actually coming out on top. Remember at 0.0001 a million shares only run you about $127.00.

  But every click will be 100$ gained. You have to wait for this to settle before you can sell them off, so remember that when your timing a sale. You can use a chart retracement to judge the future of price movement.

  So if you end up with 2 million shares that do nothing happens just wait, it might be a sleeper. It happens every once and a while but trust me it is a great feeling when you are holding a wakening sleeping gem.

 Stay tuned to what's going on in the world of your picks, keep potential plays in your watch list for quick access to them as well, in case you make money and see a good entry point.

At some point when you get your portfolio up it might be good to keep at least 1000$ dry powder in your trade balance.

You never know when you might find that last minute boomer. I am very serious about this lol, as ridiculous as it may sound. I have seen large rises and falls. In the same day. I wish more people had patience like I do so the price per share would rocket and give the company a chance to build solid roots, and establish a great company.

But with patience and a network of strong hands we can help build a strong foundation for small cap companies to thrive like supporting local businesses. But instead we win by supporting U.S. Small cap, and IPO startup companies.

High risk equals high reward for those that can endure the struggle. Waiting can be a new boat, car, or house maybe even put your kids through college.

 Investing is investing it isn't gambling. Everyone wants to make it sound crazy because it it's confusing until, you learn the language and science of it.

Remember, stay calm. Focus, think about your trades, and set your order. Re up.

Continuously search potential buys for watch list. Do your DD. If you get lost use investopiedia as a reference, they are great I love them.

Check my blog
http://pennyscryer.blogspotcom

For my current potential near break outs and long term plays.

There are thousands of penny plays, out there 80% are good, 20% pump and dump 100% pure rush of making $$$ happen on a daily basis.

If your family says that you are crazy for thinking you will make money on playing penny stocks, just tell them you are already a millionaire.

Why? Because you have a rare mindset that others cannot grasp. Investing!!

This is a rare gift my friend. Use it wisely. Warren Buffet said; "the stock market is where patient make money from the impatient." I am a firm believer of this.

It took Monster energy drink to rise from 0.60cents to $68.00 per share that is pretty amazing and worthy of the wait at those prices. Whoever put down 100-600$ is more than happy if they held for those 3 short years.

In the stocks world you have to think of 3 years is a short time frame. Because you have hard earned money invested. Like me. I write articles on the web to make money in order to trade. My money does not come easy.

But I'm blessed with a nose for hot tech stocks. That expands the little income I make from writing articles into an actual living.

Have confidence in yourself. Have faith in your research if you're not comfortable researching and doing minimal homework, and then do not waste your time trading.

Or you can always throw money into a stock you like and log out for 3 years and check on it once every three years.

Whatever the case may be, you just have to find your style that way you will trade with the fullest confidence.

When you engage with a clear mind you make wise decisions. Which is critical when investing cash into a volatile market? Don't be scared and do not let anyone scare you off. You are now a Penny Scryer.

"One that can see the future of financial potential based on candle sticks, Is one that knows the language of money."
– L.K. Cruz P.

Here are some references I like to use to find a bit about what's going on in the markets.

Allpennystocks.com – great website for screening stocks and looking at financial statements.

Penny Stock whispers – these guys can get u informed on some explosive plays.

Twitter- Yes there are some OTC pros on twitter, it's great to have a community of like minds on one thread.

I do like investor's forums as there are too many to list but there is a lot of bashing there so if you're too emotional stay clear of the forums…lol you might end up being angry u got shaken out!

Remember this is work; finding great entry & exit points are harder than it looks. This is a business so treat it like one, and it will reward you!

Good Luck Trading and don't get greedy; P